JUMPIN' JIM'

Happy Holidays

Compiled and Arranged by Jim Beloff

Foreword 3
Chord Chart 4-5

THE SONGS
All I Want For Christmas Is My Two Front Teeth 6
Baby, It's Cold Outside 8
Blue Christmas 12
The Chipmunk Song 11
Christmas Island 14
The Christmas Waltz 16
Frosty The Snow Man 18
Happy Holiday 21
Have Yourself A Merry Little Christmas 22
(There's No Place Like) Home For The Holidays 24
I'll Be Home For Christmas 26
It's Beginning To Look Like Christmas 28
It's The Most Wonderful Time Of The Year 30
Jingle–Bell Rock 32
Let It Snow! Let It Snow! Let It Snow! 34
Little Saint Nick 36
Mele Kalikimaka 38
Rockin' Around The Christmas Tree 40
Rudolph The Red-Nosed Reindeer 42
Santa Claus Is Comin' To Town 44
Sleigh Ride 46
Toyland 56
We Need A Little Christmas 50
What Are You Doing New Year's Eve? 52
Winter Wonderland 54

HAL•LEONARD® CORPORATION
7777 W. BLUEMOUND RD. P.O. BOX 13819 MILWAUKEE, WI 53213

Edited by Ronny S. Schiff
Cover and Art Direction by Elizabeth Maihock Beloff
Graphics and Music Typography by Charylu Roberts
Gibson Poinsettia ukulele photos by John Giammatteo

Foreword

In 1998 we published *Jumpin' Jim's Ukulele Christmas*, which featured our favorite Christmas carols arranged for uke. Since that time we've wanted to put out a companion songbook that would include many of the most popular and enduring twentieth-century holiday hits. If you look at the copyright information of the songs collected here, you'll note that most were written in the late '40s and '50s. This was a post-war, golden era of prosperity and optimism with expanding suburbs and the birth of the baby boom. As a result, tunesmiths were inspired to write these happy and sentimental songs, pop singers were inspired to sing them and families adopted these songs as the musical accompaniment to their aluminum Christmas trees and rooftop light shows. Sixty years later these songs have become beloved classics and one can hardly imagine a holiday season without hearing them again and again and again.

Because the Christmas season is so rich in music, it is a natural time to want to get your ukulele out and strum some favorite tunes. As usual, we've tried to set the arrangements in easy keys to play and sing, although your fingers might get a bit of a workout on songs like "The Christmas Waltz" and "Sleigh Ride."

As I write these words it is August and the thermometer is pushing into the mid-90s. Nonetheless, working on this songbook has put us in the Christmas spirit and kept us a bit cooler. Perhaps that's good enough reason to enjoy these songs at all times of the year. Here's wishing you "Happy Holidays!"

—Jumpin' Jim Beloff
August 2006

Also Available: (Books) *Jumpin' Jim's Ukulele Favorites; Jumpin' Jim's Ukulele Tips 'n' Tunes; Jumpin' Jim's Ukulele Gems; Jumpin' Jim's Ukulele Christmas; Jumpin' Jim's '60s Uke-In; Jumpin' Jim's Gone Hawaiian; Jumpin' Jim's Camp Ukulele; Jumpin' Jim's Ukulele Masters: Lyle Ritz; Jumpin' Jim's Ukulele Beach Party; Jumpin' Jim's Ukulele Masters: Herb Ohta; Jumpin' Jim's Ukulele Masters: Lyle Ritz Solos; Jumpin' Jim's Ukulele Spirit; Jumpin' Jim's Gone Hollywood; Jumpin' Jim's Ukulele Island; Jumpin' Jim's Ukulele Masters: John King—The Classical Ukulele; Jumpin' Jim's Ukulele Country; Jumpin' Jim's The Bari Best; The Ukulele: A Visual History.* **(CDs)** *Jim's Dog Has Fleas; For The Love of Uke; Lyle Ritz & Herb Ohta—A Night of Ukulele Jazz; The Finer Things: The Songs of Herb Ohta and Jim Beloff; Lyle Ritz: No Frills* **(DVDs)** *The Joy of Uke 1; The Joy of Uke 2.*

Visit us on the web at www.fleamarketmusic.com

Chord Chart

MAJOR CHORDS

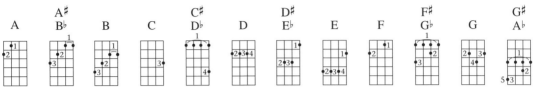

A	A# / Bb	B	C	C# / Db	D	D# / Eb	E	F	F# / Gb	G	G# / Ab

MINOR CHORDS

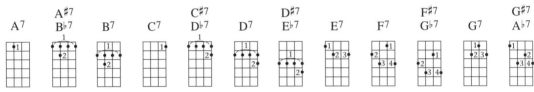

Am	A#m / Bbm	Bm	Cm	C#m / Dbm	Dm	D#m / Ebm	Em	Fm	F#m / Gbm	Gm	G#m / Abm

DOMINANT SEVENTH CHORDS

A7	A#7 / Bb7	B7	C7	C#7 / Db7	D7	D#7 / Eb7	E7	F7	F#7 / Gb7	G7	G#7 / Ab7

DOMINANT NINTH CHORDS

A9	A#9 / Bb9	B9	C9	C#9 / Db9	D9	D#9 / Eb9	E9	F9	F#9 / Gb9	G9	G#9 / Ab9

MINOR SEVENTH CHORDS

Am7	A#m7 / Bbm7	Bm7	Cm7	C#m7 / Dbm7	Dm7	D#m7 / Ebm7	Em7	Fm7	F#m7 / Gbm7	Gm7	G#m7 / Abm7

MAJOR SIXTH CHORDS

A6	A#6 / Bb6	B6	C6	C#6 / Db6	D6	D#6 / Eb6	E6	F6	F#6 / Gb6	G6	G#6 / Ab6

MINOR SIXTH CHORDS

Am6 | A#m6 B♭m6 | Bm6 | Cm6 | C#m6 D♭m6 | Dm6 | D#m6 E♭m6 | Em6 | Fm6 | F#m6 G♭m6 | Gm6 | G#m6 A♭m6

MAJOR SEVENTH CHORDS

Amaj7 | A#maj7 B♭maj7 | Bmaj7 | Cmaj7 | C#maj7 D♭maj7 | Dmaj7 | D#maj7 E♭maj7 | Emaj7 | Fmaj7 | F#maj7 G♭maj7 | Gmaj7 | G#maj7 A♭maj7

DOMINANT SEVENTH CHORDS WITH RAISED FIFTH (7th+5)

A7+5 | A#7+5 B♭7+5 | B7+5 | C7+5 | C#7+5 D♭7+5 | D7+5 | D#7+5 E♭7+5 | E7+5 | F7+5 | F#7+5 G♭7+5 | G7+5 | G#7+5 A♭7+5

DOMINANT SEVENTH CHORDS WITH LOWERED FIFTH (7th-5)

A7-5 | A#7-5 B♭7-5 | B7-5 | C7-5 | C#7-5 D♭7-5 | D7-5 | D#7-5 E♭7-5 | E7-5 | F7-5 | F#7-5 G♭7-5 | G7-5 | G#7-5 A♭7-5

AUGMENTED FIFTH CHORDS (aug or +)

Aaug | A#aug B♭aug | Baug | Caug | C#aug D♭aug | Daug | D#aug E♭aug | Eaug | Faug | F#aug G♭aug | Gaug | G#aug A♭aug

DIMINISHED SEVENTH CHORDS (dim)

Adim | A#dim B♭dim | Bdim | Cdim | C#dim D♭dim | Ddim | D#dim E♭dim | Edim | Fdim | F#dim G♭dim | Gdim | G#dim A♭dim

All I Want for Christmas is My Two Front Teeth

Words and Music by
DON GARDNER

FIRST NOTE

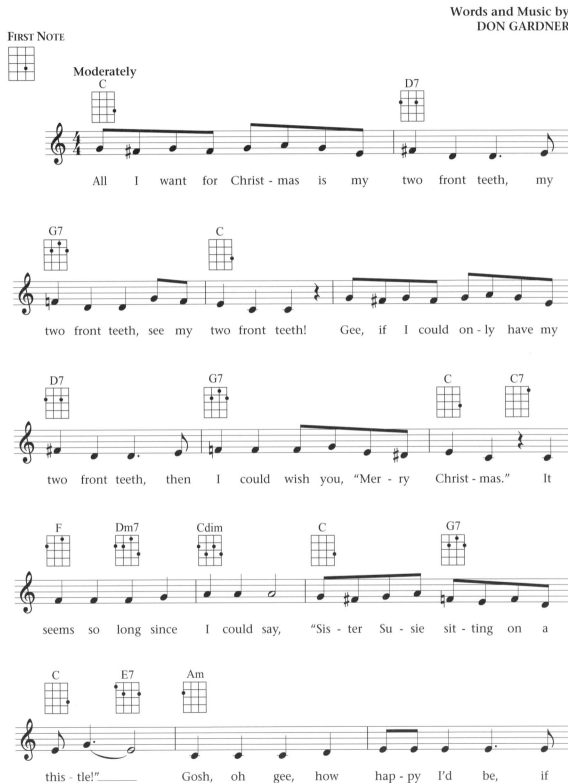

All I want for Christ - mas is my two front teeth, my

two front teeth, see my two front teeth! Gee, if I could on - ly have my

two front teeth, then I could wish you, "Mer - ry Christ - mas." It

seems so long since I could say, "Sis - ter Su - sie sit - ting on a

this - tle!"_____ Gosh, oh gee, how hap - py I'd be, if

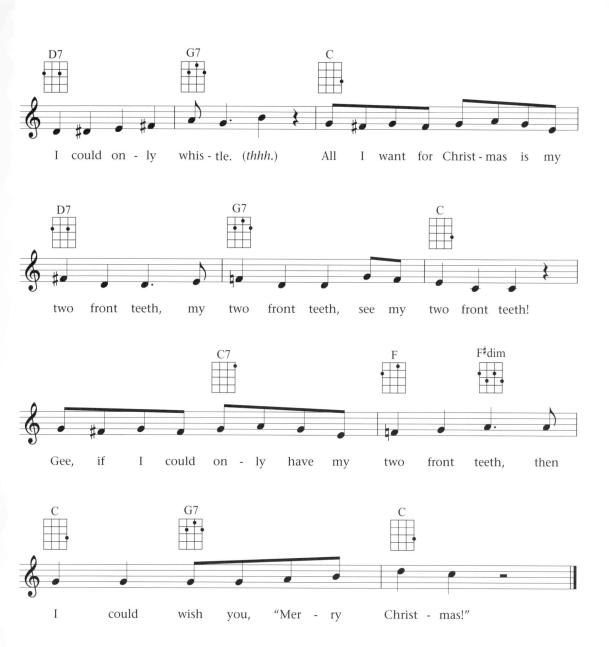

I could on - ly whis - tle. *(thhh.)* All I want for Christ - mas is my

two front teeth, my two front teeth, see my two front teeth!

Gee, if I could on - ly have my two front teeth, then

I could wish you, "Mer - ry Christ - mas!"

Baby, It's Cold Outside

By FRANK LOESSER

1. I real-ly can't stay,_____ I've the
simp-ly must go,_____ the

1. But ba-by it's cold____ out-side!____
2. But ba-by it's cold____ out-side!____

got to go 'way._____ This eve-ning has been_____
ans-wer is "no!"_____ The wel-come has been_____

But ba-by it's cold___ out-side!__ Been hop-ing that you'd_
But ba-by it's cold___ out-side!__ How luck-y that you_

___ so ver-y nice._____ My moth-er will start to
___ so nice and warm._____ My sis-ter will be sus-

___ drop in!__ I'll hold your hands,__ they're just like ice_____
___ dropped in!__ Look out the win-dow at that storm._____

F9

wor-ry____ and fath-er will be pac-ing the floor.____ So
pi-cious,____ my broth-er will be there at the door.____ My

Beau-ti-ful, what's your hur-ry?____ Lis-ten to the fi-re-place
Gosh, your lips look de - li-cious.____ Waves up-on a trop-ic-al

C6   **D7**

real-ly I'd bet-ter scur-ry.____ Well, may-be just a half a drink
maid-en aunt's mind is vi-cious.____ Well, may - be just a ci-ga-rette

roar! Beau-ti-ful, please, don't hur-ry,____
shore! Gosh, your lips are de - li-cious.____

G7   **C**   **Cmaj7**   **C6**   **Cmaj7**

more.____ The neigh-bors might think.____ Say,
more.____ I've got to get home.____ Say,

put some re-cords on while I pour.____ But ba-by it's bad____ out there.__
Nev-er such a bliz-zard be-fore.____ But, ba-by, you'd freeze__ out there.__

Dm7   **G7**   **Dm7**   **G7**   **C**   **Cmaj7**

what's in this drink?____ I wish I knew how____
lend me a comb.____ You've real-ly been grand____

No cabs to be had____ out there.__ Your eyes are like star -
It's up to your knees__ out there.__ I thrill when you touch__

9

The Chipmunk Song

Words and Music by
ROSS BAGDASARIAN

Blue Christmas

Words and Music by
BILLY HAYES and JAY JOHNSON

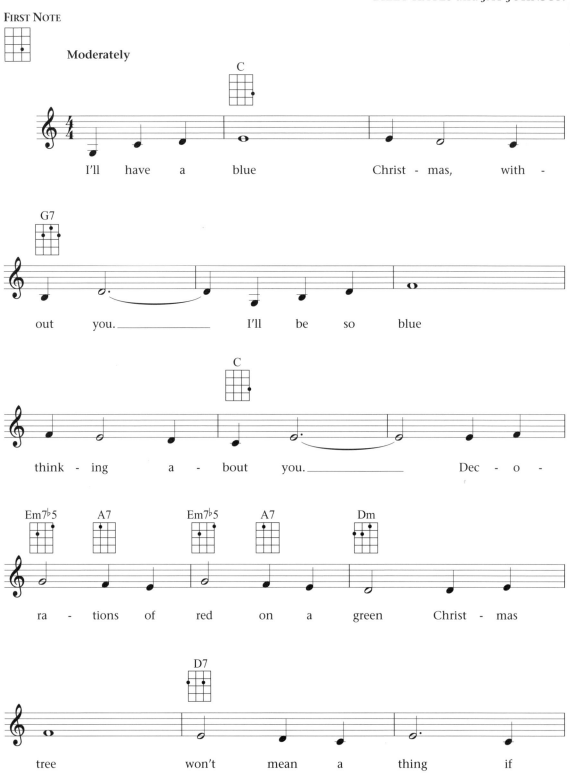

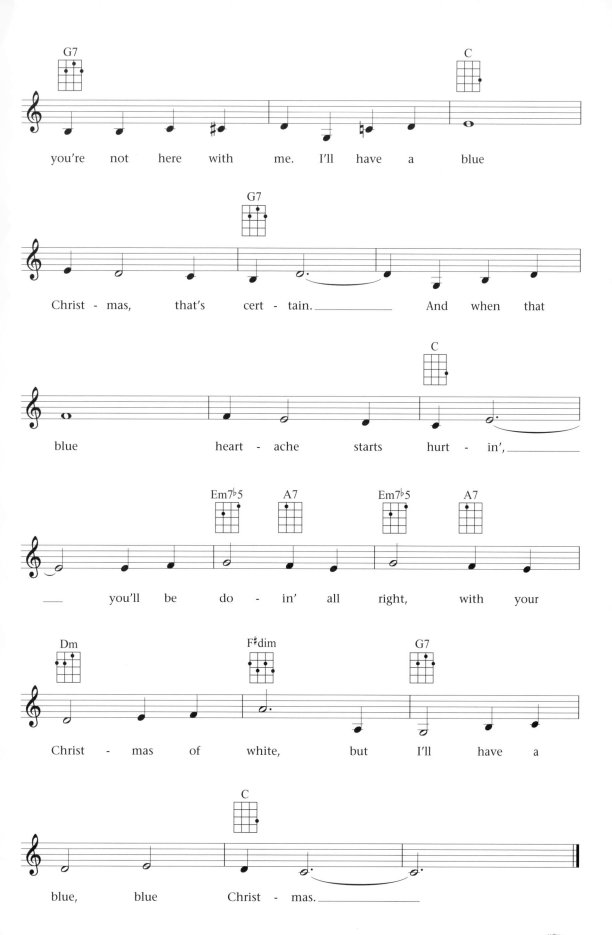

Christmas Island

Words and Music by
LYLE MORAINE

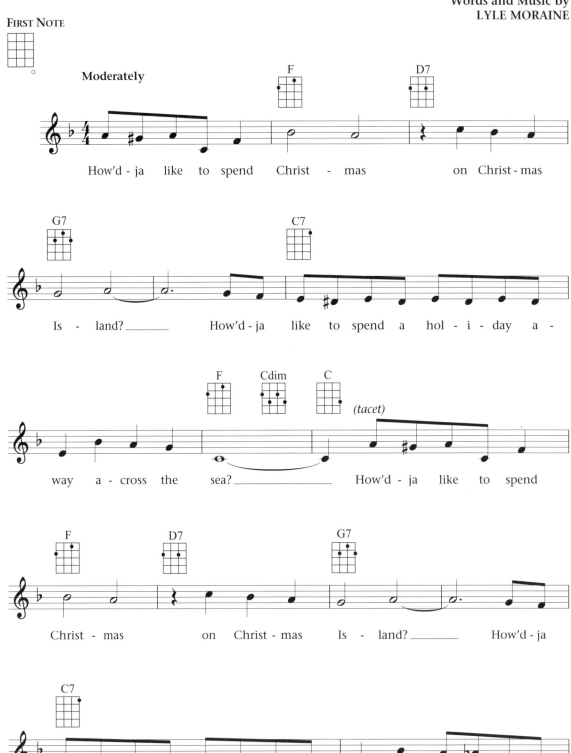

How'd-ja like to stay up late like the Is-land-ers do;_____ wait for San-ta to sail in with your pres-ents in a can-oe?_____ If you ev-er spend Christ-mas on Christ-mas Is-land,_____ you will nev-er stray, for ev-'ry day your Christ-mas dreams come true._____

The Christmas Waltz

Words by
SAMMY CAHN

Music by
JULE STYNE

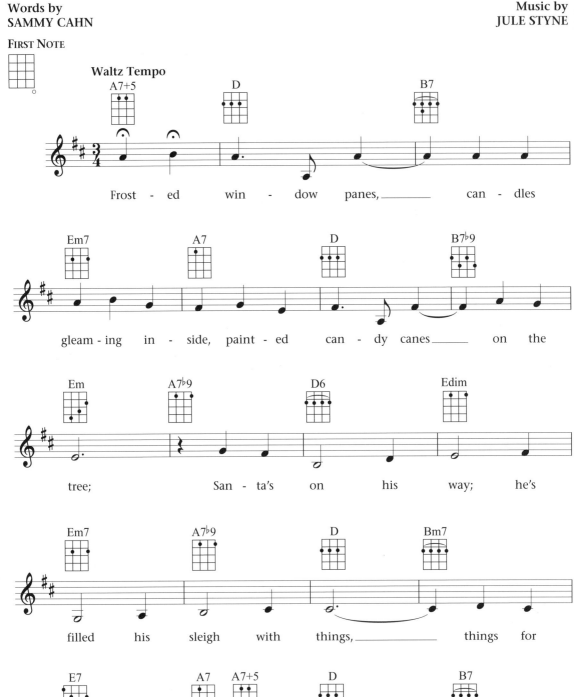

Frost - ed win - dow panes, _____ can - dles gleam - ing in - side, paint - ed can - dy canes _____ on the tree; San - ta's on his way; he's filled his sleigh with things, _____ things for you and for me. It's that time of year, _____ when the

16

world falls in love, ev-'ry song you hear _____ seems to

say: _____ "Mer - ry Christ - mas, _____ may your

New Year dreams come true." _____ And this

song of mine, _____ in three - quar - ter time, _____

_____ wish - es you and yours _____ the same thing

too _____

17

Frosty the Snow Man

Words and Music by
STEVE NELSON and JACK ROLLINS

1. Frost-y, the Snow Man was a jol-ly hap-py soul,
2. Frost-y, the Snow Man knew the sun was hot that day,

__ with a corn-cob pipe and a but-ton nose__ and two
__ so he said "Let's run and we'll have some fun__ now be-

eyes made out of coal. Frost-y the
fore I melt a - way." Down to the

Snow Man is a fair - y tale, they say,___
vil - lage, with a broom - stick in his hand,___

__ he was made of snow but the chil-dren know__ how he
__ run-ning here and there all a - round the square, say - in',

Am   D7   G   C

came to life one day. There must have been some
"Catch me if you can." He led them down the

G   Am   D7   G

mag - ic in that old silk hat they found. For
streets of town right to the traf - fic cop. And he

D   Adim   Em7   A7

when they placed it on his head he be - gan to dance a -
on - ly paused a mo - ment when____ he heard him hol - ler

D   D+   G   G7

round. Oh, Frost - y the Snow Man was a -
"stop"! For Frost - y the Snow Man had to

C   G   C

live as he could be,____ and the chil - dren say he could
hur - ry on his way,____ but he waved good - bye say - in',

Last time to Coda ⊕

G   Em   Am   D7   G

laugh and play____ just the same as you and me.
"Don't you cry,____ I'll be back a - gain some day."

19

⊕ *Coda*

G

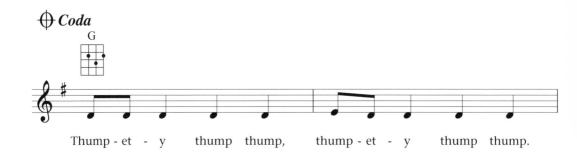

Thump - et - y   thump thump,   thump - et - y   thump thump.

D7

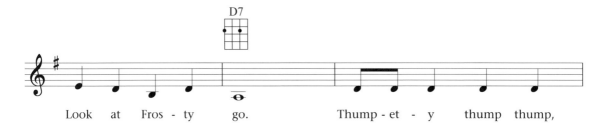

Look   at   Fros - ty   go.   Thump - et - y   thump thump,

G

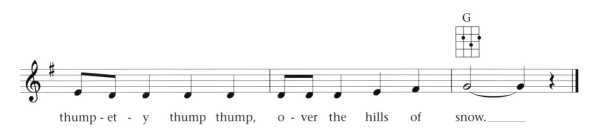

thump - et - y   thump thump,   o - ver the   hills   of   snow.____

FROSTY THE SNOW MAN

Words and Music by STEVE NELSON and JACK ROLLINS

HILL AND RANGE SONGS, INC.
BEVERLY HILLS, CALIFORNIA

Happy Holiday

from the Motion Picture
Irving Berlin's
HOLIDAY INN

Words and Music by
IRVING BERLIN

FIRST NOTE

Festively

Hap - py hol - i - day, _____ hap - py hol - i - day. _____

_____ While the mer - ry bells keep ring - ing, may your

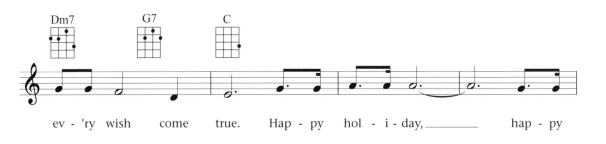

ev - 'ry wish come true. Hap - py hol - i - day, _____ hap - py

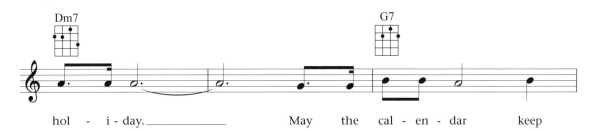

hol - i - day. _____ May the cal - en - dar keep

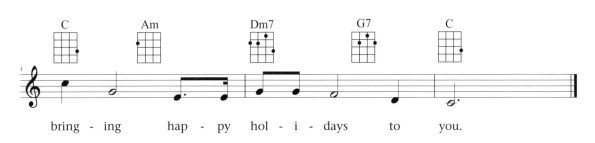

bring - ing hap - py hol - i - days to you.

Have Yourself a Merry Little Christmas

Words and Music by
HUGH MARTIN and RALPH BLANE

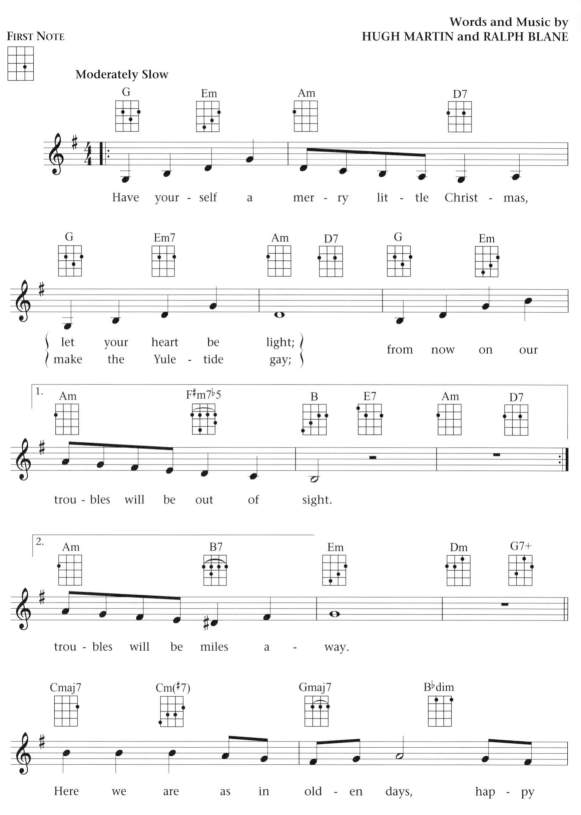

FIRST NOTE

Moderately Slow

Have your-self a mer-ry lit-tle Christ-mas,

let your heart be light;
make the Yule-tide gay;

from now on our

1.
trou-bles will be out of sight.

2.
trou-bles will be miles a - way.

Here we are as in old-en days, hap-py

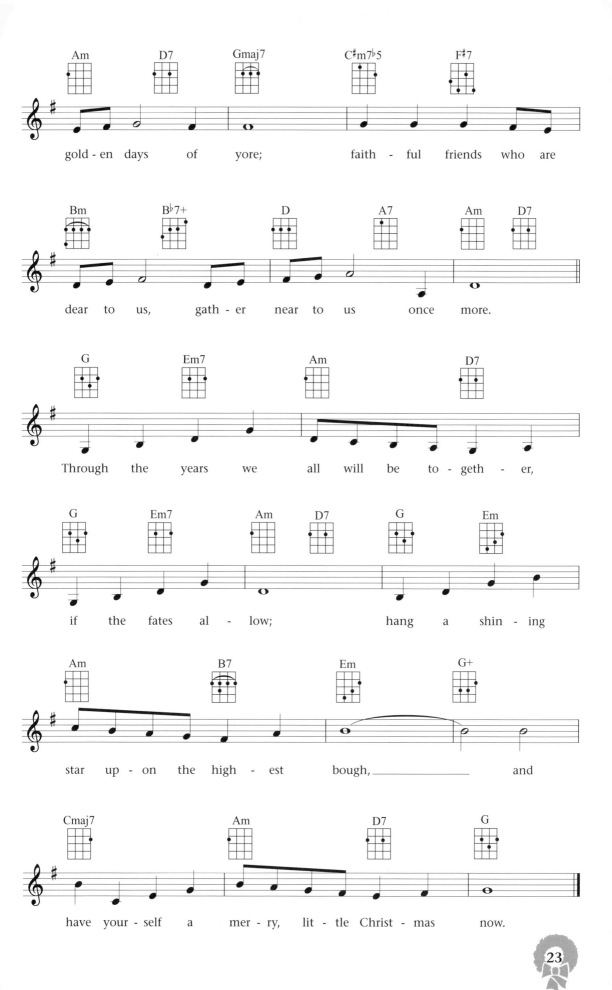

gold - en days of yore; faith - ful friends who are

dear to us, gath - er near to us once more.

Through the years we all will be to - geth - er,

if the fates al - low; hang a shin - ing

star up - on the high - est bough, _____ and

have your - self a mer - ry, lit - tle Christ - mas now.

(There's No Place Like)
Home for the Holidays

Words by
AL STILLMAN

Music by
ROBERT ALLEN

Oh, there's no place like home for the hol-i-days, ____ 'cause no mat-ter how far a-way you roam, ____ when you pine for the sun-shine of a friend-ly gaze ____ for the hol-i-days, you can't beat home, sweet home. I met a man who lives in Ten-nes-see and he was head-in' for Penn-syl-va-nia and some

24

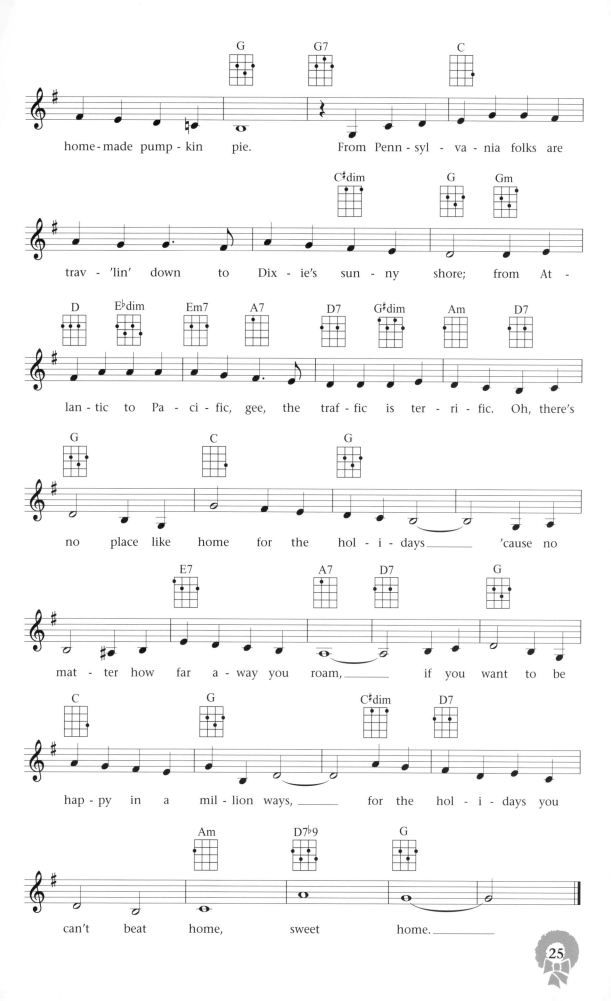

home-made pump-kin pie. From Penn-syl-va-nia folks are

trav-'lin' down to Dix-ie's sun-ny shore; from At-

lan-tic to Pa-ci-fic, gee, the traf-fic is ter-ri-fic. Oh, there's

no place like home for the hol-i-days_____ 'cause no

mat-ter how far a-way you roam,_____ if you want to be

hap-py in a mil-lion ways, _____ for the hol-i-days you

can't beat home, sweet home._____

25

I'll Be Home for Christmas

Words and Music by
KIM GANNON and WALTER KENT

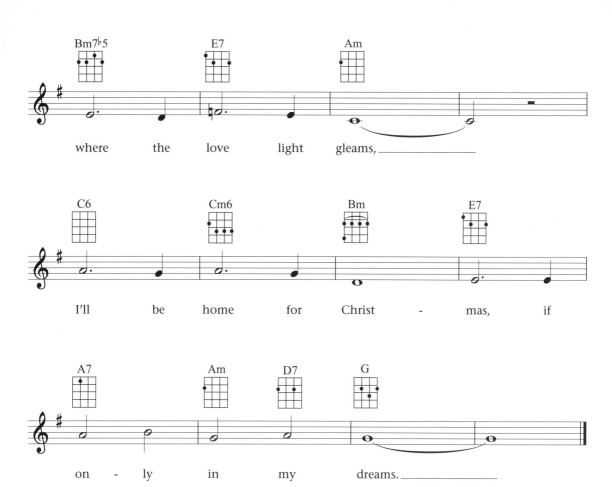

where the love light gleams, _____

I'll be home for Christ - mas, if

on - ly in my dreams. _____

It's Beginning to Look Like Christmas

By MEREDITH WILLSON

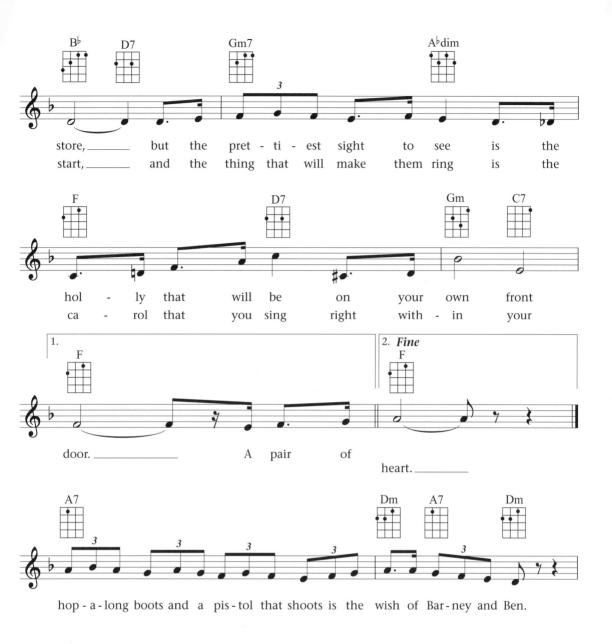

store, _____ but the pret - ti - est sight to see is the
start, _____ and the thing that will make them ring is the

hol - ly that will be on your own front
ca - rol that you sing right with - in your

1.
door. _____ A pair of

2. Fine
heart. _____

hop - a - long boots and a pis - tol that shoots is the wish of Bar - ney and Ben.

Dolls that will talk and will go for a walk is the hope of Jan - ice and Jen, and

D.S. al Fine

mom and dad can hard - ly wait for school to start a - gain. It's be -

It's the Most Wonderful Time of the Year

Words and Music by
EDDIE POLA and GEORGE WYLE

FIRST NOTE

Bright Waltz Tempo

It's the most won-der-ful time ___ of the year. ___
hap - hap-pi-est sea - son of all. ___

___ With the kids jin-gle bell-ing, and ev-'ry-one
___ With those hol-i-day greet-ings, and gay hap-py

tell - ing you, "Be of good cheer." ___ It's the most
meet-ings when friends come to call. ___ It's the hap -

won-der-ful time ___ of the year. ___ It's the
hap-pi-est sea - son of

all. ___ There'll be part-ies for host-ing, marsh-

mal-lows for toast-ing and car-ol-ing out in the snow. There'll be

scar-y ghost sto-ries and tales of the glo-ries of Christ-mas-es

long, long a-go._____ It's the most won-der-ful time_____

___ of the year._____ There'll be much mis-tle-toe-ing and

hearts will be glow-ing, when loved ones are near._____ It's the most

won-der-ful time of the year._____

Jingle-Bell Rock

Words and Music by
JOE BEAL and **JIM BOOTHE**

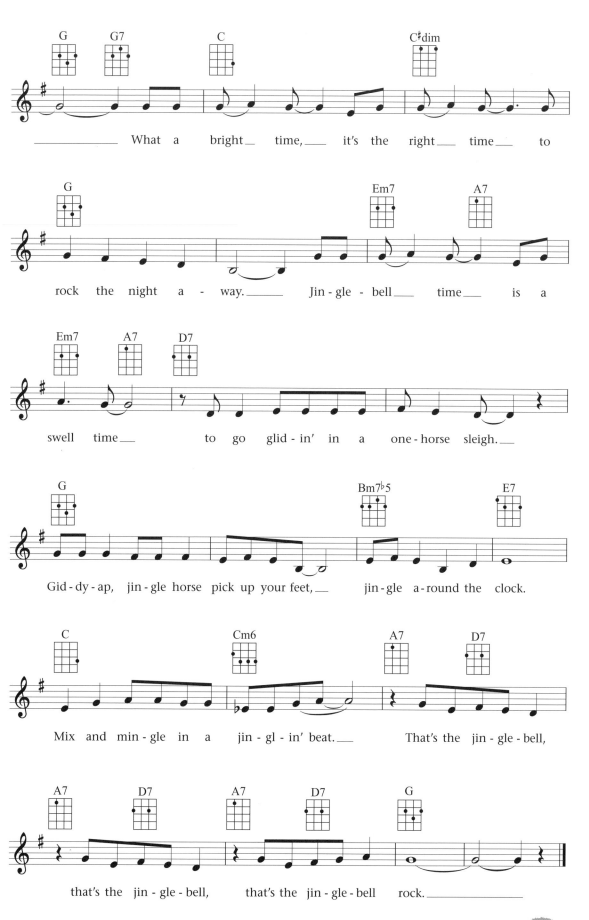

Let It Snow! Let It Snow! Let It Snow!

Words by
SAMMY CAHN

Music by
JULE STYNE

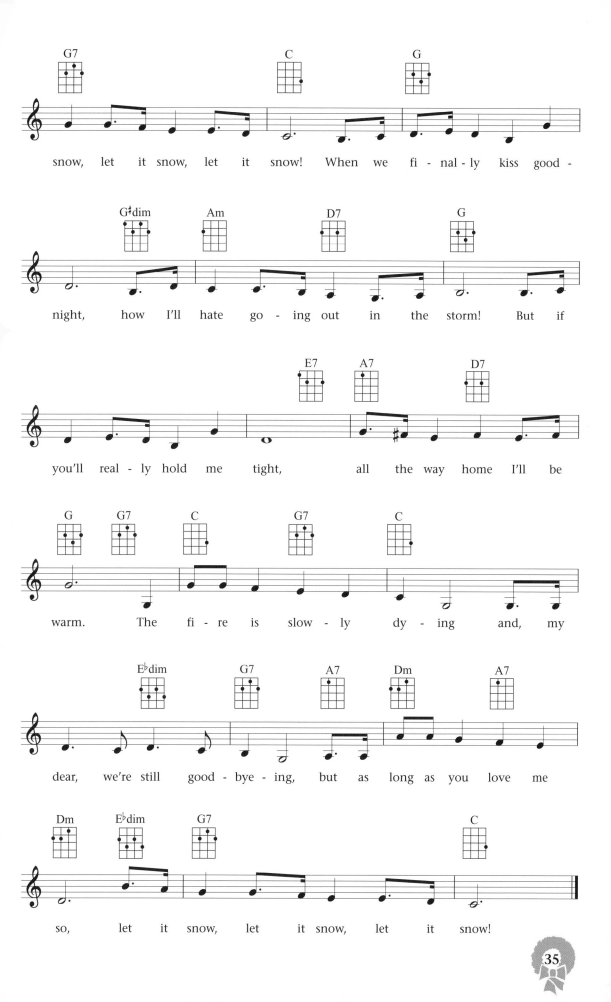

snow, let it snow, let it snow! When we fi - nal - ly kiss good -

night, how I'll hate go - ing out in the storm! But if

you'll real - ly hold me tight, all the way home I'll be

warm. The fi - re is slow - ly dy - ing and, my

dear, we're still good - bye - ing, but as long as you love me

so, let it snow, let it snow, let it snow!

Little Saint Nick

Words and Music by
BRIAN WILSON and MIKE LOVE

FIRST NOTE

Moderate rock shuffle

1. Well, way up north where the air gets cold, ___ there's a
2. lit - tle bob - sled we call it Old Saint Nick ___ but she'll
3. haul - in' through the snow at a fright - 'nin' speed ___ with a

tale a - bout Christ - mas that you've all been told, ___ and a
walk the to - bog - gan with a four - speed stick. ___ She's
half a doz - en deer with a Ru - dy to lead. ___ He's

real fa - mous cat all dressed up in red, ___ and he
can - dy ap - ple red with a ski for a wheel, ___ and when
got to wear gog - gles 'cause the snow real - ly flies, ___ and he's

spends the whole year work - in' out on his sled. ___ } It's the
San - ta gives the gas, man, just watch her peel. ___ } It's the
cruis - in' ev - 'ry pad with a lit - tle sur - prise. ___ }

Mele Kalikimaka

Words and Music by
R. ALEX ANDERSON

FIRST NOTE

Brightly

Me - le Ka - li - ki - ma - ka is the thing to say

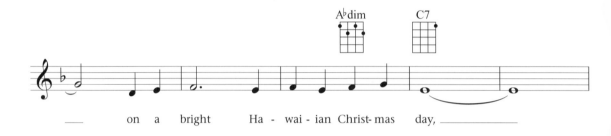

on a bright Ha - wai - ian Christ - mas day,

that's the Is - land greet - ing that we send to you,

from the land where palm trees sway.

Here we know that Christ - mas will be green and

D7

bright; the sun will shine by day and all the

G7 **C7** **F**

stars at night. Me - le Ka - li - ki -

Am7♭5 **D+** **D7** **G7**

ma - ka is Ha - wai - i's way to say Mer - ry

C7 **F**

Christ - mas to you.

Rockin' Around the Christmas Tree

Words and Music by
JOHNNY MARKS

FIRST NOTE

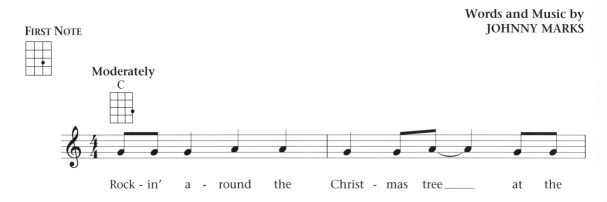

Moderately

Rock - in' a - round the Christ - mas tree ___ at the

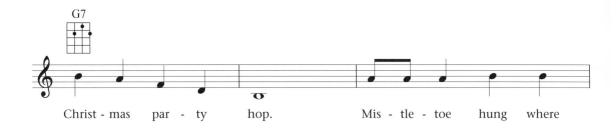

Christ - mas par - ty hop. Mis - tle - toe hung where

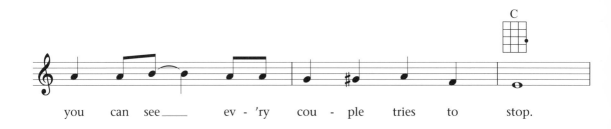

you can see ___ ev - 'ry cou - ple tries to stop.

Rock - in' a - round the Christ - mas tree, ___ let the Christ - mas spir - it

ring. La - ter we'll have some pun - kin pie ___ and we'll

Rudolph the Red-Nosed Reindeer

Words and Music by
JOHNNY MARKS

FIRST NOTE

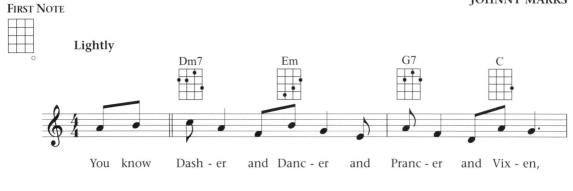

Lightly

You know Dash - er and Danc - er and Pranc - er and Vix - en,

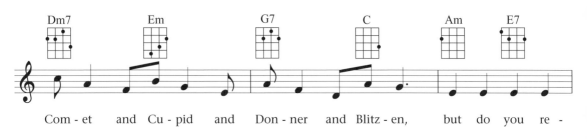

Com - et and Cu - pid and Don - ner and Blitz - en, but do you re -

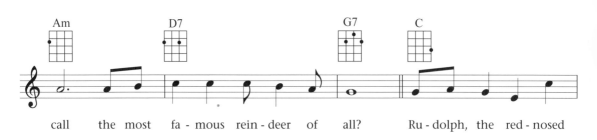

call the most fa - mous rein - deer of all? Ru - dolph, the red - nosed

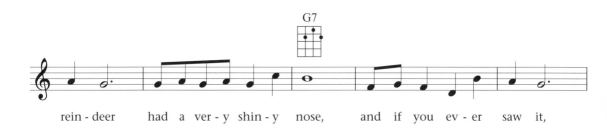

rein - deer had a ver - y shin - y nose, and if you ev - er saw it,

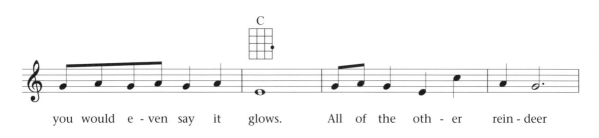

you would e - ven say it glows. All of the oth - er rein - deer

used to laugh and call him names, they nev - er let poor Ru - dolph

join in an - y rein - deer games. Then one fog - gy Christ - mas Eve,

San - ta came to say: "Ru - dolph, with your nose so bright,

won't you guide my sleigh to - night?"___ Then how the rein - deer

loved him as they shout - ed out with glee: "Ru - dolph, the red - nosed

rein - deer, you'll go down in his - to - ry."___

43

Santa Claus is Comin' to Town

Words by
HAVEN GILLESPIE

Music by
J. FRED COOTS

Sleigh Ride

Words by
MITCHELL PARISH

Music by
LEROY ANDERSON

FIRST NOTE

Moderately bright

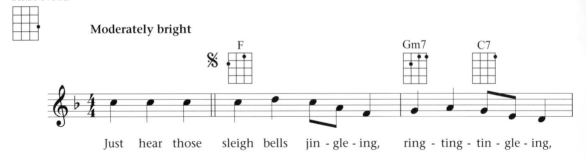

Just hear those sleigh bells jin - gle - ing, ring - ting - tin - gle - ing,

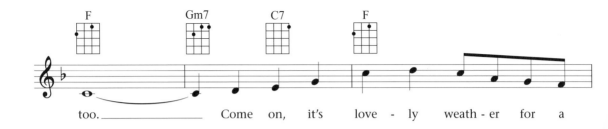

too._____ Come on, it's love - ly weath - er for a

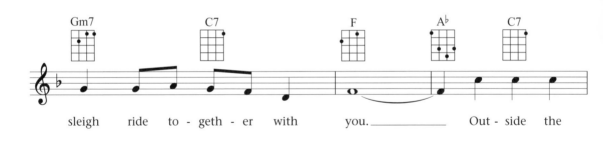

sleigh ride to - geth - er with you._____ Out - side the

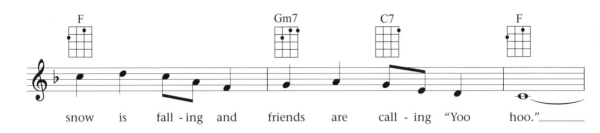

snow is fall - ing and friends are call - ing "Yoo hoo."_____

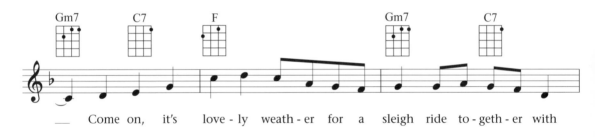

__ Come on, it's love - ly weath - er for a sleigh ride to - geth - er with

you. _____ Gid - dy - yap, gid - dy - yap, gid - dy - yap, let's go,

let's look at the show, we're rid - ing in a

won - der - land of snow. _____ Gid - dy - yap, gid - dy - yap, gid - dy -

yap, it's grand, just hold - ing your hand, we're glid - ing a -

long with a song of a win - ter - y fair - y - land. Our cheeks are

nice and ros - y, and com - fy co - zy are we, _____ we're snug - gled

up to-geth-er like two birds of a feath-er would be._____ Let's take that

road be-fore us and sing a chor-us or two,_____ come on, it's

love-ly weath-er for a sleigh ride to-geth-er with you._____

____ There's a you_____ birth-day par-ty

at the home of Farm-er Gray; it-'ll be the per-fect

end-ing of a per-fect day. We'll be sing-ing the songs we

We Need a Little Christmas

from MAME

Words and Music by
JERRY HERMAN

FIRST NOTE

Moderately bright

1. Haul out the hol - ly, _____ put up the
2. Climb down the chim - ney, _____ turn on the

tree be - fore my spir - it falls _____ a - gain.
bright - est string of lights I've ev - er seen.

Fill up the stock - ing, _____ I may be
Slice up the fruit - cake; _____ it's time we

rush - ing things, but deck the halls _____ a - gain,
hung some tin - sel on that ev - er - green

now. _____ For we
bough, _____ For I've

What Are You Doing New Year's Eve?

By FRANK LOESSER

1. May - be   it's   much   too   ear - ly   in   the   game,____
2. Won - der   whose   arms   will   hold   you   good   and   tight,____

ah,   but   I   thought   I'd   ask   you   just   the   same:____
when   it's   ex - act - ly   twelve - 'o - clock   that   night,____

"What   are   you   do - ing   New   Year's,   New   Year's   Eve?"
wel - com - ing   in   the   new   year,

New   Year's   Eve.   May - be   I'm   cra - zy

to   sup - pose   I'd   ev - er   be   the   one   you   chose

out of the thou - sand in - vi - ta - tions you'll re -

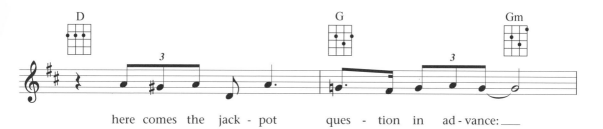

ceive. Ah, but in case I stand one lit - tle chance,___

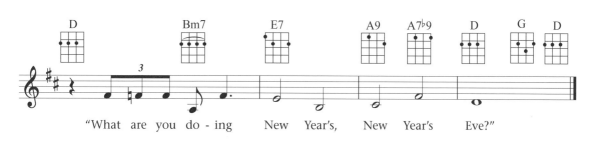

here comes the jack - pot ques - tion in ad - vance:___

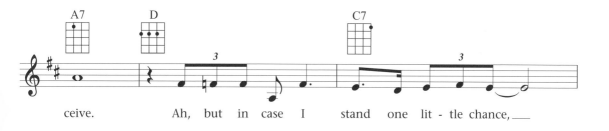

"What are you do - ing New Year's, New Year's Eve?"

Winter Wonderland

Words by
DICK SMITH

Music by
FELIX BERNARD

FIRST NOTE

Sleigh-bells ring, are you list'-nin'? In the lane snow is

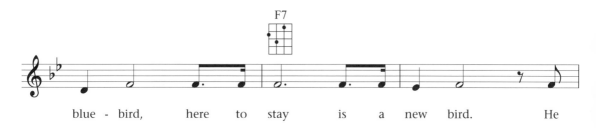

glist'-nin', a beau-ti-ful sight,___ we're hap-py to-night,___

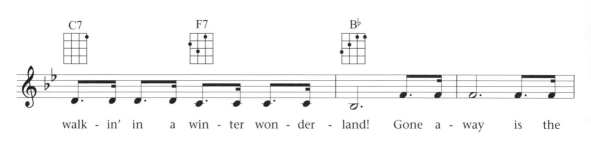

walk-in' in a win-ter won-der-land! Gone a-way is the

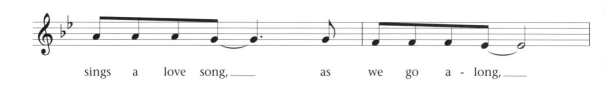

blue-bird, here to stay is a new bird. He

sings a love song,___ as we go a-long,___

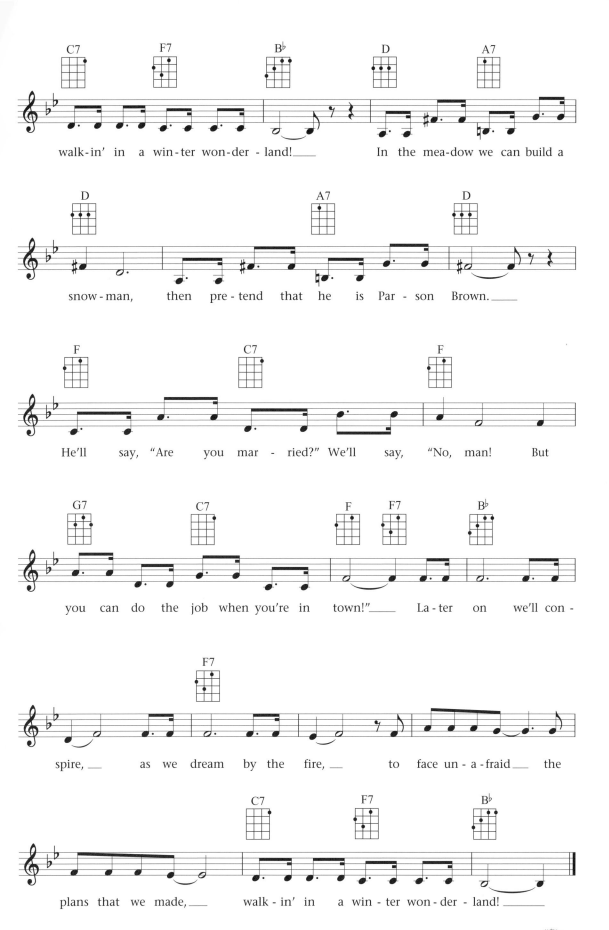

Toyland

Words by
GLEN MAC DONOUGH

Music by
VICTOR HERBERT

FIRST NOTE

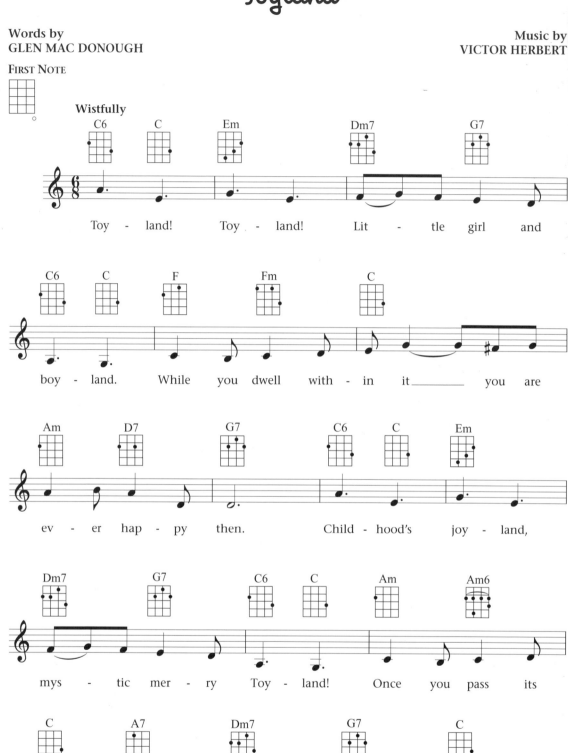

Toy - land!   Toy - land!   Lit - tle   girl   and

boy - land.   While   you   dwell   with - in   it____   you   are

ev - er   hap - py   then.   Child - hood's   joy - land,

mys - tic   mer - ry   Toy - land!   Once   you   pass   its

bor - ders   you   can   ne'er____   re - turn   a - gain.